Dandelions

This book has been reviewed
for accuracy by
Jerry Doll
Professor of Agronomy
University of Wisconsin—Madison.

Library of Congress Cataloging in Publication Data

Pohl, Kathleen.
  Dandelions.

  (Nature close-ups)
  Adaptation of: Tanpopo / Nanao Jun.
  Summary: Describes in text and photographs the
life cycle of the dandelion.
  1. Dandelions—Juvenile literature. [1. Dandelions.
2. Flowers] I. Nanao, Jun. Tanpopo. II. Title.
III. Series.
QK495.C74P547 1986   583'.55   86-26257

ISBN 0-8172-2708-3 (lib. bdg.)
ISBN 0-8172-2726-1 (softcover)

This edition first published in 1987 by Raintree Publishers Inc.

Text copyright © 1987 by Raintree Publishers Inc., translated
from *Dandelions* copyright © 1974 by Jun Nanao and Hidetomo Oda.

Photographs copyright © 1974 by Nanao-Kikaku.

World English translation rights for *Color Photo Books on Nature*
arranged with Kaisei-Sha through Japan Foreign-Rights Center.

1 2 3 4 5 6 7 8 9 0   90 89 88 87 86

Dandelions

Adapted by
Kathleen Pohl

Raintree Publishers
Milwaukee

● **Dandelions flowering by the wayside.**
Dandelions are hardy wildflowers. They grow almost everywhere, even in the most unlikely places. Dandelions are perennials, which means they live and bloom year after year.

Dandelions are one of the earliest signs of spring. These bright yellow wildflowers seem to pop up everywhere, almost overnight—in fields and pastures, on lawns, even in cracks in city sidewalks.

It is hard to imagine that at one time there were no dandelions in America. The first colonists brought dandelion seeds with them from Europe. Strange as it seems, the plant that most people today think of as a weed pest was highly valued in colonial times. Early American settlers made nutritious salads from young dandelion leaves and wine from the flowers. They ground up the plant's roots to make a coffee-like drink. Dandelion tonic was a popular remedy for the common cold and other winter illnesses.

The word dandelion comes from three French words, *dent de lion,* meaning "lion's tooth." The name refers to the plant's smooth green leaves which have deep notches that look like lion's teeth.

▶ **Frost clinging to dandelion leaves.**

In cold weather, moisture in the air crystallizes on surfaces to form frost. This rosette of dandelion leaves is covered with frost.

◀ **Ice columns reaching above the ground.**

Moisture in the earth crystallizes as columns of ice that push up from the surface of the ground.

The dandelion is one of nature's survivors. Many kinds of less hearty plants flower for only a single season, and then die. But the dandelion lives on, year after year, in spite of severe droughts or harsh winter weather.

Dandelion leaves spread out in a circle, or rosette, as they grow. This enables them to catch as much sunlight as possible. The leaves are hardy and not easily destroyed by frosts. The arrangement of leaves in a rosette also helps to protect the dandelion root from ice and snow.

The dandelion's root is called a tap root. Carrot plants also have tap roots. The orange, fleshy carrot that people eat is actually the tap root. Tap roots serve as food storage areas for plants. The food stored up in the dandelion's thick, fleshy tap root enables it to survive the winter when most other plants cannot.

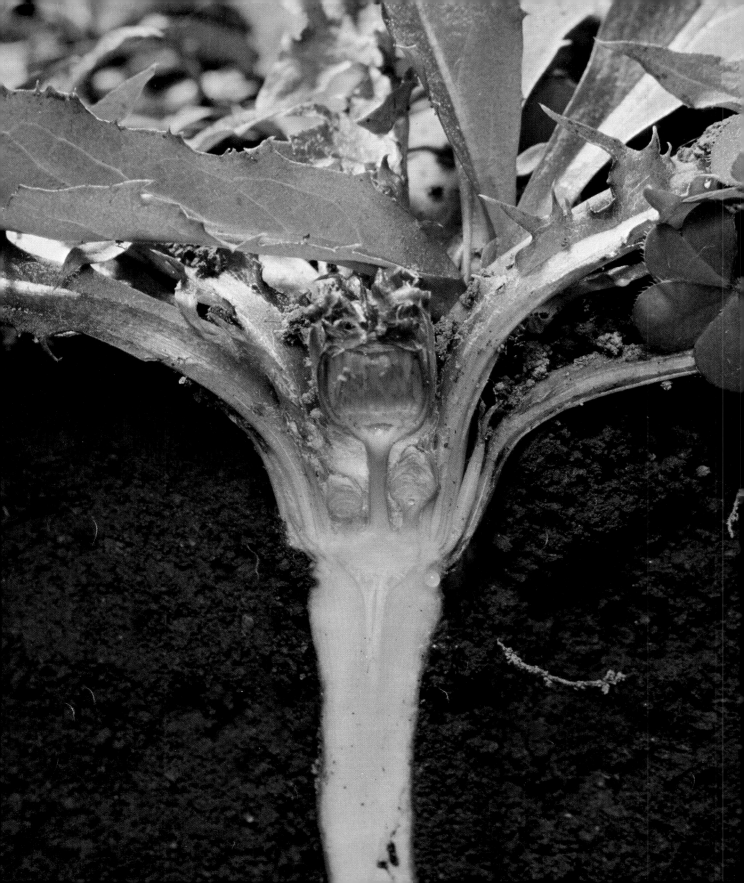

◀ **Cross-section of a dandelion plant.**

The main part of the dandelion plant is its root. The tap root grows straight down into the ground, like a carrot's tap root.

▶ **A dandelion bud in spring.**

The stored nutrients in the dandelion's root enable the plant to produce new leaves and flower buds year after year.

The main function of all plant roots is to support and anchor the plant, and to absorb water and minerals from the soil. If you have ever tried to dig a dandelion out of a lawn, you know how long the tap root can be and how stubbornly it clings to the earth. The dandelion root grows deep in the ground—it may measure two to three feet long. The long length of the root helps to protect it from frost damage, in addition to firmly anchoring the plant. Tiny, hairlike root branches grow out from the tap root. These help to absorb water and nutrients from the soil.

Soon after the snow on the ground melts in early spring, tiny flower buds begin to form on the dandelion plant.

◄ **A dandelion beginning to flower.**

The flower bud is protected by a number of green, leaflike structures called bracts. All of the bracts together are called the involucre. As the flower begins to bloom, only a single "petal," or floret, unfolds at a time.

▶ **A ladybug on a dandelion flower.**

The first warm days of spring awaken ladybugs from their winter's sleep, called hibernation. Ladybugs visit flowers to hunt, or prey upon, other insects they might find there.

Within a few days after the first tiny flower bud appears, it begins to swell up. If the days are warm and sunny, a dandelion flower soon bursts from the bud. What looks like one bright, yellow flower is actually many tiny flowers, or florets, in a cluster. There are perhaps two hundred in each cluster, or flower head. Dandelions belong to the plant family called Compositae because they have composite flowers, many tiny florets in a flower head. Daisies, thistles, asters, sunflowers, chicory, and lettuce are also members of the Compositae family.

▼**Frost on a dandelion flower.** Dandelions often flower during the first warm, sunny days of spring. Sometimes they become covered with frost, but this does not harm the flowers.

► **Flowering dandelions.**

As the temperature gets warmer, dandelion flower stalks grow longer and more and more flowers begin to bloom.

Each dandelion flower head is held up by a flower stalk, called a peduncle. It rises from the center of the rosette of leaves. Dandelion stalks are smooth, straight, and hollow. If you have ever pinched the flower from the tip of a dandelion stalk, you may have noticed the milky white substance that oozes out. This sticky juice has latex in it, a material used in making rubber. Scientists have tried to make rubber from the milky dandelion juice, just as they have from the milky juice of rubber trees. But so far, they have not been very successful.

Most people think of the flower stalk as the dandelion's stem. But the stem itself is actually very short and usually grows only about a half inch above the ground. As is true of other plant stems, it serves as a kind of transportation system. It carries water and minerals that are absorbed from the soil by the roots to the plant's leaves. And it carries food that is produced by the leaves to other parts of the plant.

In the warm, sunny days of early spring, many fields and lawns seem to become completely carpeted with bright yellow dandelion flowers. Because dandelion leaves grow close to the ground, the plants grow best in open areas, where they don't have to compete with tall plants for sunlight.

Dandelions, like all green plants, need sunlight in order to make food for themselves. The green leaves of plants combine energy from sunlight with carbon dioxide and water to produce food. This complex process is called photosynthesis. The word *photosynthesis* means "to produce with light."

As the plant leaves are making food, the dandelion's flower stalk grows very quickly. It may reach a foot high in just a few days' time. As the stalk grows taller, the flowers are raised high off the ground. This is important to the plant. The tall stalks make it easier for the dandelion seeds to be scattered, or dispersed, by the wind, which means that new dandelion plants can take root in new places.

◄ **Dandelions blooming in a field in spring.**

Dandelions can often be found in orchards, pastures, and hay fields, and on people's lawns.

● **A honeybee on a dandelion flower.**

This honeybee collects plant pollen in pollen baskets on its back legs. The plant pollen is good food for honeybees and other insects. When the bee visits another flower, some of the pollen will brush off on it. In this way, bees and other insects help pollination to take place.

Flowers are important to plants because they produce seeds from which new plants grow. Each tiny dandelion floret has both the male and female parts necessary to produce a new seed. The female flower part is a long, thick tube, called the pistil. The tip of the pistil is called the stigma. The long, narrow neck is the style. At the base of the pistil is the ovary, where the eggs are located. The male part of the flower is called the stamen. It has yellow tips, called anthers, which contain tiny dustlike grains of pollen. The pollen grains enclose the male sperm cells.

In order for new seeds to form in most kinds of plants, a process called pollination must first take place. Pollination occurs when a pollen grain from an anther touches the stigma of a pistil. Both insects and the wind help pollination to take place.

But dandelions are one of the few plants that can form fertile seeds (from which new plants can grow) when pollination has not occurred at all. In fact, scientists believe most new dandelion seeds are formed in this asexual way. Each flower head can produce 150 to 200 seeds. So it is no wonder that dandelions are able to multiply so quickly in fields and on lawns.

18

● **A cluster of dande-lion flowers (left photo) and a single floret (right photos).**

The dandelion flower is actually a cluster of tiny, individual flow-ers. What seems to be the single petal of each floret is actually five petals fused to-gether. All of the petals together on a flower make up the corolla.

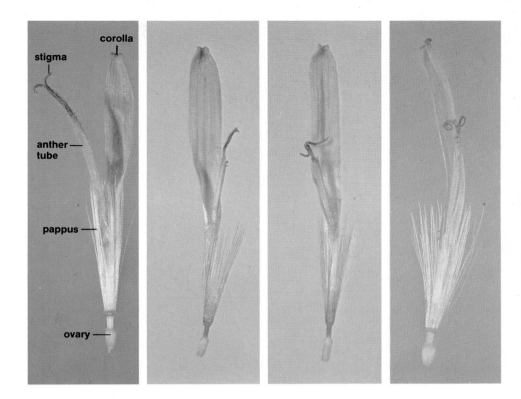

If you were to take a single dande-lion floret from a cluster of flowers, you would see the parts that are shown in the photo above. At the base is the rounded ovary, where the seed will form. The circle of fine white hairs above the ovary is called the pappus. The long, yellow tube that grows out from the pappus is the anther tube. The plant's stamens have joined together at their tips to form the anther tube, which encloses the female pistil. The yellow flower "petal" that you see is actually five petals fused together. The petal be-gins to move away from the anther tube as the floret opens up.

The dandelion flower dispenses its pollen in a most unusual way. The anthers release their pollen in-side the anther tube. The style of the pistil grows upward through the tube, brushing the pollen along with it. Finally, the pollen is pushed out the tip of the anther tube. Some of it is carried, by insects or the wind, to other dandelion plants. Only then does the stigma, the tip of the pistil, uncurl its tips. It is ready to receive pollen from another dandelion plant. This is called cross-pollination.

If cross-pollination does not take place for some reason, the dandelion may eventually pollinate itself. The stigma will form a loop and curl around until it touches any pollen that might remain on the outside of the anther tube.

Often, insects help plant pollination to take place. Bees, butterflies, and other insects are attracted to the brightly colored petals of dandelions and other flowers. They are also attracted to the plants' pollen and nectar.

Nectar is secreted by plants especially to attract insects. The sweet-tasting nectar has lots of sugar in it. It gives insects the energy they need to move around.

Plant pollen is rich in protein. It has the same food value for insects that meat and eggs have for people.

As insects flit from flower to flower, they carry grains of pollen with them on their bodies. The pollen brushes off on other flowers, pollinating them. Plants and insects help each other out in this way.

But dandelions rely less on insects for pollination than many other plants because they are able to reproduce without pollination taking place at all.

◄ **Various kinds of insects are attracted to the brightly colored dandelion flowers.**

(1) A small copper butterfly drinking plant nectar. (2) A dronefly. (3) A long-horned beetle (left) and bird lice (right). These insects eat both plant pollen and the flower petals. (4) A praying mantis nymph lying in wait for an insect to come near. (5) A crab spider which has caught a mosquito. (6) A skipper butterfly drinking nectar with its long, strawlike proboscis.

▶ **At dusk, the dandelion closes its flowers.**

Dandelion flowers open up in bright sunlight. They remain partly closed on cloudy days. They also close up at night.

● Withered dandelion flowers (left) and a dandelion which has lost its flowers (below).

Once the tiny flowers have been pollinated, they begin to shrivel and die. But the flower stalks of the plant continue to grow upward. The achenes and pappi remain protected inside the involucre after the flowers have fallen off.

Once a dandelion floret is pollinated, the pollen grain absorbs sugar and water from the stigma on which it has landed. It swells up and sends a tube down the long neck of the pistil. When the pollen grain reaches the ovary, it releases a sperm, which joins with an egg. A seed begins to form from the fertilized egg.

As the seed develops, it receives nutrition from the dandelion plant. It remains enclosed in the ovary, which eventually hardens and dries out. The small, dried-up fruit (ovary) which contains the dandelion seed is called the achene. Each achene has a long, silklike pappus attached to it. The pappus will serve as the parachute when the achene is launched on the wind.

Within several weeks, the dried-up flower parts on the dandelion stalk will fall from the plant. But the achenes, with their long pappi, remain enclosed in the involucre. All of the achenes together make up the seed head of the dandelion.

▼ **The dandelion seed head begins to open.** Both the stalk and the involucre supply nutrients for the developing seeds. Soon, the bracts bend back and the heads of the pappi begin to spread out.

◄ **Fluffy dandelion seed heads.**

Each pappus in the seed head has raised its parachute and is ready to be lifted into the air.

▶ **Dandelion parachutes.**

The dandelion has developed a very special way of dispersing its seeds in many directions.

Once the dandelion seed head is fully formed, the bracts of the involucre begin to bend back. The head of each pappus begins to spread out, forming the parachute that will lift the achene into the air. Soon, all the pappi in the seed head have raised their parachutes. The seed head looks like a fluffy white blowball.

The stalk of the dandelion contin- ues to grow rapidly as the seeds are developing. The taller the stalk, the more likely it is that each dandelion parachute will be lifted by a gust of wind. As the wind carries the dandelion parachutes, it scatters them far and wide. Each parachute carries a seed from which a new dandelion plant can grow.

◀ **A dandelion seed head that is almost bald.**

Just one achene remains to be parachuted away from this dandelion seed head. The bracts of the involucre have outlived their usefulness. They begin to wilt.

▶ **An ant carrying a dandelion seed and parachute.**

This ant is struggling to carry a dandelion achene with the parachute still attached. The ant will add the seed to its store of winter food in its nest.

Once all the achenes have parachuted from the dandelion flower stalk, it begins to wither and die. Its job of carrying nutrients to the flowers and raising the seeds high in the air is finished. But although the stalk and flowers of the plant have died, the tap root and leaves live on. They will continue to support life for the dandelion plant year after year, as new leaves and stalks form and new flowers and seeds develop.

Many of the dandelion achenes that are scattered by the wind never grow into new plants. Some will land in rivers, lakes, and streams. Others will be carried to rocky cliffs or dropped on stone walls or rooftops. Many will be eaten by insects and other animals. But some of the seeds will land on good soil. They will escape the watchful eye of hungry animals. They are the seeds that will take root and grow into new dandelion plants.

When an achene does land on the ground, its parachute usually falls off. The achene has tiny hooks in it that help keep it anchored to the soil so that it won't be washed or carried away. But sometimes, the pappus remains attached to the achene after it lands. Then, if a strong wind gusts along, it may pick up the achene and take it to a different place.

If the seed lands on soil, and if the weather conditions are right, the seed coat will split open and the seed will sprout, or germinate. The sprout will form the tap root of the new dandelion plant. It will develop tiny root hairs to absorb water and nutrients from the soil. Soon seed leaves will push up through the soil and tiny flower buds will appear. And a whole new crop of dandelion plants will be blooming in the spring.

◄ **An achene that has fallen into the water.**

Some achenes simply land in the wrong places and are not able to grow into new plants.

● Taking root and budding.

The achene splits open as the seed begins to sprout (lower photo). A seed that has fallen on the ground needs very little moisture before it begins to sprout. That is why dandelions are able to grow even between the cracks in sidewalks. Soon, seed leaves appear aboveground (photo inset).

Let's Find Out

Where Do Dandelions Grow?

Dandelions like sunny areas. They do not grow well in dark forests or in places where the grass is tall. That is because the leaves of tall plants block out the sun. If dandelions don't get enough sun, they can't produce food for themselves, and will not be able to form seeds and flowers. But if there is enough sunlight, a dandelion will grow even on a high mountain.

Comparing the Heights of Dandelions

In milder climates, dandelions may flower even in the winter. These dandelions cling to the ground; their flower stalks are very short. In spring, when plants around them start to grow, the dandelions' leaves and flower stalks grow higher.

Dandelions in early spring.

Dandelions at the end of spring.

There Are Different Types of Dandelions.

Taraxacum albidum, found in West Japan.

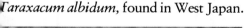

The Latin name for the dandelion commonly found in the United States is *Taraxacum officinale*. It has two rows of bracts. The outer row is bent downward and does not move. The upper row of bracts moves to open and close the flower and seed head. In Japan, there are about twenty types of dandelions.

Taraxacum officinale, native to Europe.

Taraxacum japonicum, native to Japan.

Playing with Dandelions

Dandelion Straws

The stalk of the flower is hollow, like a straw. Break off a dandelion stalk and use it to blow bubbles.

Dandelion Whistles

Cut a stalk and lightly crush one end with your teeth. Then blow through the crushed end to make a whistling sound.

GLOSSARY

achene—a dried fruit which contains a single seed. (pp. 22, 28)

asexual—a nonsexual way of reproducing. (p. 16)

bracts—the green leaflike structures that protect the flower bud and seed head of the dandelion. (pp. 10, 31)

composite—many small flowers clustered together, which look like a single large flower. (p. 10)

floret—a tiny flower, usually one of many in a flower head. (pp. 10, 19)

pappus—fine, silklike hairs on the dandelion achene which help to parachute it into the air. (pp. 19, 22)

perennials—plants that live and bloom year after year. (p. 4)

photosynthesis—the complex process by which green plants make food, with the help of chlorophyll, a substance found in the plants' leaves, and energy from sunlight. (p. 15)

pollination—the process in which pollen is transferred from an anther to the tip, or stigma, of a pistil. (pp. 16, 19)

rosette—a cluster of leaves arranged in a circle. (p. 6)

tap root—the fleshy, main root of carrots, dandelions, and some other plants, which serves as a food storage area. (pp. 6, 9)